The Little Guide to
BIG Success

12 STRAIGHTFORWARD LESSONS TO SUCCEED AT ANYTHING!

RICH LOHMAN

The Little Guide to BIG Success
12 Straightforward Lessons to Succeed at Anything!

Printed in USA
Paperback ISBN: 979-8-9910479-1-3
Hardback ISBN: 979-8-9910479-0-6

This book is dedicated to YOU, the reader. To the person YOU were, the person YOU are, and the person YOU are becoming.

To become the best version of yourself, you will need to grow. You have likely heard these lessons before. I want to challenge you not to think, "I have heard this before!" Rather, I want to encourage you to think, "How well am I doing regarding this lesson?"

Wishing YOU much success in your journey!

"The plans of the diligent lead to profit as surely as haste leads to poverty." —Proverbs 21:5 NIV

"Dig into almost every overnight success story and you'll find about a decade's worth of hard work and perseverance." —Austin Kleon

Table of Contents

Introduction

Success means different things to different people. While some people think they are unworthy of it, others are confused by what they think it is. And some have even become very frustrated by the pursuit of their definition of success because they aren't seeing the outcomes they desire fast enough. But one thing is certain, the process to achieve noteworthy success is similar for everyone, and that process is what we will explore in this book.

I've written this book for one purpose, and one purpose only: to help you, the reader, achieve the results and potential that you have in your life. If I can play a small part in your journey by helping you apply the lessons I have in this book, it will be enough for me to be fulfilled and satisfied that I have done my part to help you.

These lessons have helped me immeasurably over my lifetime and continue to help me to this day. As a matter of fact, these lessons continue to help me as I write this book. I have found myself stuck in several places where I'm pressed up against these lessons in my very own journey to writing my first book. Knowing where I am at in the journey and what is required to move past each point to successfully publish this book is part of the process. You will have your own journey of success. When you do, I hope this book and these 12 simple lessons will give you a pathway to success. I wrote this to encourage you and inspire you to follow the process to achieve your dreams.

The journey won't always be easy. Life is messy and has many twists and turns for all of us. However, I believe you can find where you are in your journey by reflecting on these lessons. I also believe that when you know where you are on your journey, you can create a plan from where you are, to where you want to be and what you want to achieve.

If at any point in your journey, you get stuck and you are struggling, I, as a speaker, coach, and leadership and personal development trainer, would be honored to help you more than the book may be able to. Please reach out to me and engage in a conversation when needed. This book would help me reach out and help more people. However, some people will need an extra helping hand or a little bit of coaching, and if that's you, I want to encourage you to reach out via our website at www.project1202.com. It would be our honor to meet you, help you, guide you, and lead your potential.

Mark Twain eloquently stated, "Twenty years from now you will be more disappointed by the things you didn't do than by the ones you did. So throw off the bowlines, sail away from the safe harbor. Catch the tradewinds in your sails."

Are you ready to change your life for good? Then, let's get started!

LESSON 1
Show Up . . . Every Day

*"I feel strongly about showing up and being prepared
and not taking the opportunity for granted and being
conscientious about my fellow co-workers."*
—Paul Schneider

There's an old saying that goes, "Eighty percent of success is showing up." Simple, isn't it? Yet, most of us tend to underestimate the power of this seemingly insignificant act.

Success, in any form, begins with the choice to show up—every single day. Consider a seed planted deep within the earth. It doesn't sprout overnight. Instead, it shows up daily, embracing sunlight and rain alike, until one day, it blooms into a magnificent flower or fruit-bearing tree. Likewise, we must learn to "show up" if we wish to achieve our dreams.

What Does "Showing Up" Mean?

Showing up is about more than just being physically present. It requires engaging mentally and emotionally. It's about bringing your A game each day—being prepared, focused, and ready for whatever life throws at you.

Being mentally prepared is about focused thinking on your

success image (vision), success drivers (goals), and the activities and people that will help you achieve your best results.

Unfortunately, most people lack mental preparedness because they are more focused on how many likes they got on their recent post, the drama in their social media feeds, or the countless reels & TicToks they have already watched that day.

One way is showing up with total mental control over the outcomes they are after. The other is showing up so distracted that success is like finding a needle in the haystack, at best.

To be emotionally prepared means to have emotional goals each day. Coming out of Covid, I was really struggling with my emotional control. I found myself to be angry, outraged, or exhausted in many situations and with many people. I grabbed a 3X5 index card and started using it as a bookmark in the book I was reading. Each day I opened the book, I looked at the index card to determine my emotional goals for the day. On one side, I wrote "decrease anger, rage, and exhaustion," on the other side, I wrote, "increase energy, passion, peace, and drive." Each day I looked at my calendar, married up my emotional goals and deter-mined how I would decrease the bad emotions and increase the good ones. Over time I found myself showing up in a better emo-tional state each day. To this day, I practice showing up focused on the right emotional state.

The Benefits of Showing Up Daily

1. **You start living up to your potential sooner.** When you con-sistently show up each day to work toward your goals or dreams, you progress faster than someone who shows up

only once in a while. Therefore, you begin realizing your true potential far earlier.

2. **Your confidence increases.** As you show up and engage in regular practice or effort, you witness yourself becoming more reliable and disciplined over time. This makes you feel good about yourself.

3. **Your relationship with your body and mind improves.** Regardless of the goal, showing up requires mental and/or physical activity. Being active strengthens your physical health and/or mental well-being over time, which further supports overall success.

4. **You attract more good into your life.** Putting in consistent effort towards achieving goals attracts similar energies back into our lives. This is often referred to as the Law of Attraction.

5. **You are ready for opportunities when they come.** Being consistently active puts you in a prime position to grab hold of new opportunities when they come along.

Of course, showing up is not always easy. There will be days when you would rather stay in bed than face the world. When your motivation is low, every task feels like climbing Mount Everest.

What do you do then? You still show up!

How to Show Up Daily

1. **Expect it to be hard.** Remember that success isn't meant to come easy. If it were, everyone would have achieved it. This

is probably the most difficult thing for most people to do. Think about it: if we expect it to be hard, we might not want to even begin in the first place. This requires a big mindset shift. When you learn to make the shift, you will embrace the difficulties because you know that all growth, all challenges, and the best results come from doing something outside your comfort zone.

2. **Remember your whys.** Keep reminding yourself of why you started in the first place; this will keep your motivation level high. I call this "why-power." The more whys you have, the stronger your why-power will be to challenge yourself, change, and improve how you show up. Most people only have one or two reasons why they are doing something. When the why isn't strong enough, the way forward is more difficult. When you have ten, twenty, or thirty reasons why you want and need to do something, those whys will replace your need for willpower. Willpower is temporary; why-power is long-lasting because it is attached to your purpose, your mission, and your image of yourself as a successful person.

3. **Be prepared for negative beliefs.** Our minds often play tricks on us by feeding us negative thoughts or excuses—don't buy into them!

4. **Start coaching yourself.** Make a list of your strengths and capabilities, and look at it regularly.

5. **Get a coach or other source of outside perspective.** Sometimes we need someone else's perspective to motivate us and keep us focused on our goals. The Bible verse Matthew 5:16 encapsulates this beautifully: "In the same way, let your light shine before others, that they may see your good deeds and glorify your Father in heaven."

Remember, every journey begins with a single step. Marathon runners don't think about the finish line right from the start. Instead, they focus on the next step, and then the next—because, added together, those steps are what get the runner towards their goal. Similarly, focusing on showing up each day should be our primary approach towards achieving any long-term goal!

Consistent effort leads to success.

So here's my challenge for you today—show up! Whether it's a workout session, a business meeting, or that personal project you've been putting off—just show up and give it your best.

You might be surprised at the power of this simple act!

Reflection Questions

1. What stood out to you from this lesson to help you?

2. What do you need to do to be more consistent at showing up daily?

3. Which of the suggested ways to show up daily do you commit to putting into practice?

Work Hard

"Success isn't always about greatness. It's about consistency. Consistent hard work leads to success. Greatness will come."
—Dwayne "The Rock" Johnson

Life is a journey that unfolds in surprising ways, and it's often the most challenging paths that lead us to our greatest destinations. One of those paths is hard work.

When you hear the phrase *hard work*, what comes to mind? Is it long hours, sweat on your brow, or perhaps a sense of achievement?

In reality, hard work encompasses all these elements and more. Hard work isn't just about labor—it's also about perseverance, resilience, dedication, and self-discipline. It's about pushing past limits and breaking barriers.

But why do we put so much emphasis on hard work? Why not seek shortcuts or easier routes? Because hard work has real benefits.

The Benefits of Hard Work

1. **It makes you a better person.** Over time, doing your utmost builds character—each challenge faced shapes us into stron-

ger and more disciplined individuals.

2. **It advances your career or grows your business.** In a world where most seek easy solutions, hard work stands out. This visibility can open up new opportunities as people recognize your commitment and dedication.

3. **It's satisfying.** Hard work gives you a daily sense of pride and achievement.

A story that perfectly illustrates this is Colin O'Brady's 2018 crossing of Antarctica solo and unaided by wind power—a feat deemed impossible by many experts before his attempt. His determination and relentless training led him to finish an unimaginable 932-mile journey across frozen wastelands—all alone—in fifty-four days!

> *"Whatever you do, work at it with all your heart, as working for the Lord, not for human masters[.]"*
> —Colossians 3:23 NIV

Evidence can be found everywhere for the importance of hard work—from leading CEOs who rose from humble beginnings, such as Howard Schultz (Starbucks) or Ursula Burns (Xerox), to athletes like Serena Williams, who have dominated their sports through sheer willpower and ceaseless practice.

Consider Thomas Edison's famous quote: "Genius is one percent inspiration, ninety-nine percent perspiration." Edison himself was no stranger to grueling labor—he performed 2,774 failed experiments before he succeeded in inventing the incandescent light bulb. His story serves as a powerful example of how relentless effort can lead to pioneering discoveries.

How to Cultivate an Outstanding Work Ethic

1. **Treat your body right.** Eat a proper diet, exercise regularly, and get plenty of rest. Without a healthy body, maintaining high levels of productivity becomes challenging.

2. **Eliminate distractions.** Schedule blocks of time for work, family, and relaxation, and stick to that schedule as much as possible. Multitasking is notoriously inefficient; it is far better to be focused and present for each activity.

3. **Look for opportunities for improvement.** Like an athlete training for a competition, measure your efforts against others in your field to gauge where you stand and what further steps are needed to improve.

4. **Be dependable.** Set personal standards for yourself that transcend those set by society or your peers. Commitment is just as important as hard work itself.

5. **Don't get discouraged when you hit a stumbling block.** Remember: every journey has its ups and downs. Expect to make mistakes and encounter problems. Each one is a learning opportunity and a stepping stone towards greater achievements. Among the myriad facts and statistics on this topic, one study conducted by psychologist Angela Duckworth stands out: her research found that grit—a combination of passion and perseverance—is a significant predictor of success.

By fostering these qualities within yourself, you'll become more flexible and better equipped to handle whatever comes your way each day.

> "Genius is one percent *inspiration*,
> ninety-nine percent *perspiration*."
> —Thomas Edison

Of course, you don't want to be like a car spinning its wheels, working hard yet achieving nothing. So how do we ensure our work is effective?

How to Work Effectively

1. **Set clear goals.** For work to be effective, you need to know what you are working toward.

2. **Develop a plan that details the steps necessary to achieve each goal.** The plan may change as obstacles arise, but it is still important to have a plan.

3. **Then take action!** Begin with small tasks related to your goals, and gradually build up from there while remaining consistent in your efforts (remember Colin O'Brady).

Hard work offers more than just material rewards. It shapes character, instills discipline, opens doors to new opportunities, and ultimately paves the way to success. So roll up those sleeves and get to it!

The journey might be tough, but remember:

> "*The only place where success comes
> before work is in the dictionary.*"
> —Vidal Sassoon

Reflection Questions

1. What stood out to you from this lesson?

2. How will you cultivate a strong work ethic?

3. Of the 3 steps to work more effectively, which one do you need to do a better job of implementing?

Try New Things

*"You never know what you can do until you try,
and very few try unless they have to."*
—C.S. Lewis

magine standing at the edge of a cliff, staring down into an abyss filled with shadows and uncertainty. It's scary, right? You don't know what might be down there!

But consider this: within those shadows could be undiscovered treasures—experiences that may change your life for the better.

The Benefits of Trying New Things

1. **It makes you smarter.** Research has shown that engaging in new activities can improve brain function, enhance memory, and strengthen cognitive abilities.

2. **It boosts confidence.** Accomplishing something we've never done before gives us a sense of achievement, making us feel good about ourselves.

3. **It's fun!** Trying new things keeps life interesting and exciting; it's like adding spices to a bland dish.

> Trying new things improves brain function, broadens our perspective, increases self-confidence, and keeps life interesting.

So how do we go about it?

How to Try New Things

1. **Identify behaviors that need changing or enhancing.** Is there something holding you back from reaching your full potential? Recognize it. Then add it to a "Do Something" list—not a wish list, but an action list filled with things you want to try or achieve.

2. **Let go of limiting beliefs.** You know those nagging thoughts that say, "I can't"? Chuck them out because guess what: You CAN!

3. **Plan and execute.** Don't just say, "I'll do it someday," because someday often turns into never.

4. **Start paying attention to your gut feelings.** They're usually right. If something feels right, go for it! Conversely, if it doesn't feel right, hold back.

It's important to remember that Rome wasn't built in a day. Start small and gradually increase the intensity or duration of the new activity.

*"Forget the former things—do not dwell on the past.
See, I am doing a new thing! Now it springs up—
do you not perceive it? I am making a way in the
wilderness and streams in the wasteland."*
—Isaiah 43:18–19 NIV

In life's wilderness of uncertainty and challenges, trying new things could be your path forward—your personal stream that leads you through the wasteland and towards success. Step forward bravely! After all, every successful person has dared to try something different at some point in their journey towards success.

Reflection Questions

1. What stood out to you from this lesson?

2. What do you think is preventing you from trying new things?

3. Which of the steps given for trying new things will you commit to help you?

Fail

*"Failure should be our teacher, not our undertaker.
Failure is delay, not defeat. It is a temporary detour, not
a dead end. Failure is something we can avoid only by
saying nothing, doing nothing, and being nothing."*
—Denis Waitley

It may seem counterintuitive that a book about how to succeed includes a chapter dedicated entirely to failing. In a world that presents success as the ultimate goal, we often overlook the hidden virtues of failure. Yet, it's through our failures, our stumbles and falls, that we truly learn how to succeed.

Let's try an experiment. Think back to a time when you failed at something. Recall the negative feelings you had at the time. Now switch your perspective and imagine that failure as a best friend who was looking out for you.

Sound odd?

Stay with me here.

Whenever we try something new or challenging, there's always a risk of failing. And it's okay to fail. The brain learns through trial and error, constantly adapting and restructuring neural connections based on experiences. Each time we fail, it pushes us outside our comfort zone and forces us to evolve and grow stronger—mentally and emotionally.

Science backs this up, too. A study conducted by Stanford University demonstrated that students who were taught about learning from failures performed significantly better than those who weren't.

A great example lies within nature itself. Consider a sapling growing on the forest floor. Older trees tower above it, their leaves forming a canopy that blocks out most of the sunlight. The sapling doesn't give up, though. It pushes upwards towards the sun despite its difficult circumstances, constantly reaching for its goal, until one day it breaks through from beneath those giants casting shadows upon it and basks in glorious sunlight!

That's resilience!

Do you remember learning how to ride your first bike? What if, after falling once or twice, you had decided never to try again? Would you be able to ride today? Probably not!

Hopefully I've convinced you failures are just stepping stones leading you to success. Like a piece of coal that, under immense pressure, turns into a diamond over time, enduring repeated failures can transform you into a resilient warrior ready to face life's challenges. But unlike the coal, you must take an active role.

How to Learn From Failure

1. **Acknowledge each failure.** Failure does not define you, so don't be afraid to admit failure. Rather than blaming a failure

on someone or something else, own it.

2. **Learn from the failure.** Your perspective shapes your interpretation of failure—use it as a chance to evolve. Analyze what you could have done differently. Seek advice from books or mentors.

3. **Keep moving forward.** Remember what Denis Waitley rightly said: "Failure is delay, not defeat." Persistence in the face of failure leads to greater resilience.

Failures are just stepping stones leading you to success.
Like a piece of coal that, under immense pressure,
turns into a diamond over time, enduring repeated
failures can transform you into a resilient warrior.

Remember, everyone fails at times. What's important is how we rise after falling. So when life knocks you down seven times, stand up eight! By reframing our view on failures, we enable ourselves to extract valuable lessons hidden within them, which ultimately propels us towards our goals.

Reflection Questions

1. What stood out to you from this lesson?

2. How can you reframe how you view failure to use it as a tool for your success?

3. What is one step you can take to use failure as a tool for your growth?

LESSON 5

Improve

"You make the world a better place by making daily improvements to become the best version of yourself."
—Roy T. Bennett

The concept of self-improvement isn't new. Philosophers have been pondering its importance for centuries. Epictetus wrote, "Progress is not achieved by luck or accident, but by working on yourself daily."

To improve oneself isn't merely about gaining new skills or knowledge. Rather, it encompasses a holistic approach towards understanding oneself better and striving for a more meaningful existence.

Indeed, much of what truly leads to happiness and fulfillment is rooted in personal improvement. A study published in the Journal of Personality and Social Psychology found that people who were committed to personal growth experienced higher levels of psychological well-being compared to those who weren't.

Benefits of Personal Improvement

1. **It increases your self-awareness.** Personal improvement requires getting to know yourself: your strengths and weaknesses, your values, and your priorities.

2. **It gives you a sense of direction.** When you know yourself, you can set clear goals for yourself that are in line with your values.

3. **It increases focus and effectiveness.** By improving, we give ourselves the permission to focus on getting better at something that will likely help us achieve our goals. When our focus is on becoming a better version of ourselves, we eliminate distractions that sabotage our progress towards our goals.

4. **It provides motivation.** Every step we take towards our goals motivates us to keep moving forward.

5. **It enhances resilience.** I believe in a quote my mentor, John Maxwell, shared with me repeatedly. He said, "Anything worthwhile is uphill. Uphill dreams require uphill habits." When we develop those uphill habits, we build our resilience to keep driving forward.

6. **It fosters more fulfilling relationships.** Self improvement is attached to self-worth. The better we feel about ourselves, the more we can give to others. I often tell people you cannot give what you do not have. Relationships are more fulfilling when you have something to give to people, and self-improvement is the key to the process.

7. **It boosts confidence and self-esteem.** Simply put, it's hard to feel bad about yourself when you are getting better at something.

8. **It can enhance job security.** According to an article published in *Harvard Business Review*, employees who engage in lifelong learning are less likely to get automated out of their jobs.

Personal improvement doesn't happen overnight—
it requires commitment and persistence.

The science behind self-improvement reveals some interesting facts. Research shows that our brains possess an inherent ability, known as neuroplasticity, that allows us to learn new things and adapt to change throughout our lives. This is why we're capable of constant growth and transformation if we put our minds to it.

Successful people from various fields have also vouched for the significance of personal development in their lives. For instance, Oprah Winfrey once stated that she considers her entire life as an ongoing classroom where she learns more about herself every day. She has also said, "If you want your life to be more rewarding, you need to change the way you think."

Now that we've established the importance of improving oneself, here are specific steps you can take.

How to Identify Areas for Improvement

1. **Practice mindfulness.** Being present at each moment helps you understand yourself better, which aids in self-improvement. Examples of mindfulness include breathing exercises, meditation, praying, gratitude, journaling, amongst others.

2. **Cultivate emotional intelligence.** Emotional Intelligence tests assess your strengths and weaknesses in 5 core areas: Self-Awareness, Self-Regulation, Empathy, Decision-Making, and Social Skills.

Self-awareness is the knowledge of one's own thoughts, feelings, and motivations. The more in tune you are with your thoughts and your willingness to change your thoughts, the more you can improve your results. The more you can target desired feelings and avoid unwanted feelings, the better your results will be. Understanding your motivations, strengthens your drive and resolve to achieve great things.

Self regulation is the ability to manage emotions and actions in various environments. Regulating emotions, especially in stressful environments, is a direct predictor of one's ability to be successful. With emotions under control, actions and/or reactions can be directed toward the desired outcomes.

Empathy is the capacity to understand, empathize and appreciate another perspective. Not a single one of us is perfect and others may have perspectives that are better than ours. Our ability to empathize and appreciate others will determine our success level.

Decision-making is the ability to make responsible choices and accept the outcomes. Some people are more decisive or impulsive than others, while others are more methodical and slow in decision-making. Everyone can improve their decision-making by reflecting on decisions and evaluating the outcomes. If you don't like your outcomes, you need to change your decisions. One of the best ways to do this is to ask yourself, "Who or what will be negatively impacted by this decision tomorrow?" This question can slow down the decision-making process and give everyone a new perspective on the decision being made.

Social skills are important because they help us create and maintain healthy relationships. Healthy relationships are significant in all areas of our lives because life isn't meant to be done alone. I heard it once said, "Nothing of significance is ever done alone". Having the social skills to seek help and assist others is crucial to our long-term success.

3. **Learn something new every day.** This could be anything from reading a book or taking up an online course related to your field of interest. It can also come from being present in every conversation and practicing listening and asking good questions. When learning becomes a core focus, growth starts to take place.

4. **Seek feedback.** Constructive criticism provides valuable insights into how you can improve further. So don't shy away from criticism. Seek it out by asking others how you can do better.

   If you are anything like I used to be, you might think feedback and criticism are bad. It took me studying the value of criticism to realize its benefits. When taken correctly, you become wiser, gain better judgment, improve your listening skills and better analyze the feedback. You can also help others live a better life by sharing the feedback you have received.

5. **Set clear goals.** Identify what areas you want to improve upon—whether it's enhancing your communication skills or becoming more organized. Goals simply become targets you want to arrive at through activities and they help you stay focused on what you want instead of focusing on things you don't want.

   Once you've identified areas in which you want to improve, you need a strategy for improving.

How to Improve

1. **Test**. Nothing happens until we attempt to do something. Taking action is the first step of improvement because it gives us an outcome to evaluate. Rarely do we get something right the first time, so it is likely there will be mistakes.

2. **Fail**. Again, we will likely make mistakes early on in anything we do. We live in a culture where failure is demonized as bad, and we try to prevent it altogether. The problem with this is that we learn the most from our mistakes and failures. And it's worth noting that if you aren't failing, then you are likely playing it safe, limiting the extent of your success. So take bigger risks. Be okay with failure and you will see your biggest gains follow.

3. **Learn**. This is the process by which you evaluate your mistakes objectively. Simple questions in a time of evaluation, like the following, are crucial to your learning:

   What went right?

   What went wrong?

   What could I have don't more of?

   What should I have done less of?

   What could I have done better or differently?

4. **Improve**. Taking your answers from your learning time reflection questions and turning them into a specific, measurable, timed plan is a crucial step in the process.

5. **Reenter**. The last step is to get back in the game and make another attempt at the outcomes you desire. Wayne Gretzky

is famous for saying, "You miss 100% of the shots you don't take." So get back in there and take more shots at the success you desire.

Maintain a journal: Writing down your
thoughts and reflecting on them regularly
can help track your progress over time.

Remember, Rome wasn't built in a day. Personal improvement is a lifelong journey, not a destination. You might not see immediate results, but rest assured, every effort counts in your pursuit of becoming the best version of yourself.

"For the Spirit God gave us does not make us fearful,
but gives us power, love and self-discipline."
—2 Timothy 1:7 NIV

Stay committed to your goals, be patient, and keep moving forward one step at a time!

Reflection Questions

1. What stood out to you from this lesson?

2. Which area of improvement will be the most important for you to focus on right now?

3. What will you do to commit to the improvement process of Test, Fail, Learn, Improve, & Reenter?

LESSON 6

Grow

"It takes courage to grow up and become who you really are."
—E.E. Cummings

*Take chances, make mistakes. That's how you
grow. Pain nourishes your courage. You have
to fail in order to practice being brave.*
—Mary Tyler Moore

What does it mean to grow as a person?

Growth is not about improving one's skills or performance. Nor is it about trying new things—although trying new things can lead to growth.

Growth is about evolving your perspective and expanding your horizons. When it comes to perspective, I use the DISC Behavioral Styles report to aid my understanding. The four basic styles are D for Dominant, I for Influencer, S for Steady, and C for Contemplative. Each of these styles has a predictive perspective by which they view any topic. Let's say the topic is leadership (one of my favorite topics to teach and talk about). Each style responds according to the following perspectives:

D style people hear leadership and think, "WHAT" do they need to do?

I style people hear leadership and think, "WHO" am I leading or WHO is involved?

S style people hear leadership and think, "HOW" do I do leadership?

C style people hear leadership and think, "WHY" are we talking about leadership?

Our goal in growth is to be able to grow and see all the different perspectives, WHAT, WHO, HOW, and WHY and use the perspective that best helps us get closer to the results we want.

The Benefits of Growth

1. **You'll have more options to choose from in life.** Broadening your perspective exposes you to new ideas and new applications of ideas.

2. **You'll be more motivated.** New ideas are exciting, and excitement boosts motivation.

3. **You'll be happier.** Studies in psychology show that people who continuously strive for personal development tend to be happier than those who remain stagnant.

4. **You'll improve your career prospects.** Knowing about other cultures makes you a more valuable employee. Moreover, the ability to see an issue from multiple perspectives is a valuable skill in any endeavor.

5. **You'll improve your interactions with others.** Growth makes a person more empathetic to the experiences of others, which enhances all kinds of relationships.

6. **You'll be more confident.** According to a study by *Harvard Business Review*, people who actively seek opportunities for growth are 142% more likely to feel confident in their ability to continuously learn and grow.

Eager to get started? Consider these common growth opportunities. And keep in mind that personal growth sometimes requires stepping outside your comfort zone.

Areas for Growth

1. **Emotional.** This kind of growth involves adding to your toolbox of methods for managing stress, cultivating a positive outlook on life, improving your attitude, and managing anger.

2. **Mental.** This means exercising your mind to stay open to new ways and ideas.

3. **Physical.** This kind of growth can be summed up as learning better ways to eat and exercise.

4. **Cultural.** This kind of growth entails seeking out experiences outside your current cultural milieu.

5. **Spiritual.** This does not necessarily mean religion, but rather how you perceive the world around you and the impact you can have on it.

6. **Financial.** Financial growth is not simply growing your nest egg, but growing in the way you handle your money and debt.

> *"Live a life worthy of the Lord and please him*
> *in every way: bearing fruit in every good work,*
> *growing in the knowledge of God [. . .]."*
> —Colossians 1:10 NIV

Growth is holistic. Just like a tree needs sunlight, water, air, and nutrients for nourishment and survival, humans need emotional support, mental stimulation, physical wellness, social interaction, spiritual fulfillment, and financial stability.

Trees branch out in all directions: upwards towards the sun, downwards into the earth for stability, and sideways to reach out to others. Be like a tree and grow in all directions!

Venturing into uncharted territories allows us to meet different kinds of people and become part of diverse communities. It exposes us to various perspectives, broadening our understanding of life itself.

Be like trees and grow in all directions: Emotional, Mental, Physical, Cultural, Spiritual, Financial

---

Let's take Steve Jobs as an example. He was known for his insatiable appetite for seeking knowledge, staying open-minded, and being willing to take risks. His relentless pursuit of innovation ultimately led him to create a wildly successful suite of innovative products such as the Macintosh computer, iPod, iPad, and iPhone. His journey exemplifies how continuous learning and experimentation can lead one to unparalleled success.

Now that we've comprehensively discussed the concept of growth, let's study specific steps you can take to foster your own personal growth.

How to Grow

1. **Identify areas where you want to grow.** For some ideas, refer back to "Areas for Growth" earlier in this lesson.

2. **Seek out new information and experiences** in the areas you've identified. For example, you might invite a colleague from another department to lunch, read a book or take a class about something you wish you'd learned in school, or try a sport or fitness activity that is entirely new to you.

3. **Set goals and monitor your progress.** As with any goal, when you find an idea you wish to implement in your life, set a clear, measurable goal, develop a plan to achieve the goal, then revisit the plan regularly and adjust it when needed.

4. **Stay open-minded.** Not every new idea will be one you want to use in your daily life, and that's fine. But, to maximize the benefits of growth, be flexible and willing to adapt.

5. **Know that the rewards of growth may not be immediate.** Steve Jobs audited a calligraphy course during college. Although it was not pertinent to his intended degree (and he dropped out of college anyway), this experience inspired him to develop the first affordable WYSIWYG fonts and software for Macintosh computers.

Personal growth is a process. Growth is not linear; it often involves setbacks and challenges. Especially when you are learning something very new, regular and consistent practice is essential for progress. Stay curious, be adaptable, and enjoy the journey, knowing you will reap benefits.

36

Reflection Questions

1. What stood out to you from this lesson?

2. Which benefit do you want to experience in your growth and why?

3. Which areas of your life do you want to grow right now, and how will you accomplish it?

Overcome Hardships

*"No person can become strong without struggle,
without the effort of pitting himself against trouble
and hardship. And to meet and deal with life creatively
we will always need to be alert and thoughtful and
to think in a positive manner, constantly rallying
personality forces into effective and desirable action."*
—Dr. Norman Vincent Peale

Every journey includes some hardships. Struggle is universal—it's not limited by geography or socioeconomic status.

Hardships are not fun, but they have a hidden utility that becomes clearer as the dust settles. They act as catalysts for growth and transformation, pushing us beyond our comfort zones into uncharted territories where real growth happens. In retrospect, many successful people attribute their achievements to trials they've faced.

When we talk about hardship, it's essential to understand what it means at its core. It's more than simply facing challenges or problems—it involves enduring despite them, even when giving up seems like the easier option.

The Benefits of Hardships

1. **Hardships build character.** You learn the importance of empathy and compassion when you go through hardship. If you have ever experienced a flat tire on the side of the road and a good samaritan stopped to help you change the tire, you not only felt gratitude for that individual but also experienced compassion in that moment. That simple example also teaches you empathy towards others and the hardships they may be experiencing. Hardship teaches us to appreciate the support from others and hopefully return the favor to someone else one day.

2. **Hardships make you experienced.** When you persevere through hardship, you become more valuable in your profession—because you have seen things others have not.

3. **Hardship is a learning opportunity.** Navigating hardship often requires creative problem-solving, thereby teaching you what to avoid in the future. It also teaches you resilience, a skill in itself.

Research by S.R. Maddi in 2006 suggested that people who perceive hardships positively exhibit higher levels of psychological resilience—a crucial factor in overcoming adversity successfully.

Consider, also, how many times Thomas Edison failed on the way to inventing the incandescent light bulb: 2,774 times, according to his own records.

It's clear that embracing failure can pave the way for unparalleled success.

To navigate through hardships effectively requires taking

deliberate steps toward personal development.

Hardships act as catalysts for growth and transformation, pushing us beyond our comfort zone into uncharted territories where real growth happens.

How to Navigate Hardships Effectively

1. **Accept the reality of the hardship.** Acknowledge the hardship and don't shy away from it.

2. **Reflect on it.** Understand what caused the hardship and how you can learn from it. Seek advice.

3. **Take action.** Implement a plan based on learned lessons to prevent recurrence—or to better manage the situation if it occurs again.

A case study that exemplifies this process is Steve Jobs' infamous firing from Apple. He accepted his situation, reflected on his mistakes, and returned to Apple with a broader perspective, ultimately leading the company to new heights.

Now on to the meaty stuff. Hardships are inevitable, but you can leverage them towards achieving success.

How to Overcome Hardship

1. **Change your perception of adversity.** See each struggle as an opportunity for growth.

2. **Cultivate resilience.** We all react to stress in different ways, and often our reactions are counterproductive. Some people quit at the first sign of trouble. Others look for a scapegoat, or become angry, or become anxious. Identify your counterproductive responses to hardship, then work on them with the help of books or counseling. The resilience you learn will help you bounce back stronger after every setback.

3. **Practice mindfulness.** Mindfulness is the habit of being fully present in the moment, aware of where we are and what we are doing, and learning not to overreact or get overwhelmed by what is going on around us. Mindfulness helps in accepting situations beyond your control so you can focus on the areas where you can make positive changes.

4. **Find support.** A strong support system acts as your safety net during tough times. It could be friends, family, or even professional counseling services.

5. **Celebrate small victories.** This boosts your morale, helping you stay motivated during difficult times.

> *"Blessed is the one who perseveres under trial because,*
> *having stood the test, that person will receive the crown of*
> *life that the Lord has promised to those who love him."*
> —James 1:12 NIV

Remember, no matter how challenging things may seem right now, the storm always passes, leaving behind clear skies and renewed strength. Embrace these trials with open arms because they are preparing you for the success story waiting just around the corner.

Reflection Questions

1. What stood out to you from this lesson?

2. What must you do to better navigate the hardships you experience more effectively?

3. What will you do differently to overcome your hardships and challenges?

Handle Rejection

*"Remember, the pain of rejection is nothing
compared to the pain of regret."*
—Matthew Hussey

Rejection. It's a word that sends chills down most people's spine.

Whether it's from a prospective employer, a romantic interest, or even a friend, rejection can feel like a gut punch.

But does it surprise you that facing rejection could be one of your greatest tools for success?

Let's take a step back and look at this from another angle. You've probably heard the phrase "What doesn't kill you makes you stronger." It might sound cliché, but there is profound truth in those words, especially when applied to dealing with rejection.

J.K Rowling was rejected by twelve publishers before the manuscript that became *Harry Potter and the Philosopher's Stone* was accepted and became an international sensation.

Rejection often feels like the end of the world, but in reality, it's just the beginning of finding your true path. Every *no* brings you closer to the ultimate *yes*.

The Benefits of Rejection

1. **It's a chance to regroup and refocus.** The hardships and rejection we experience tend to take us away from where we intended to go in the first place. But as face rejections, it allows us to slow down and regroup. When regrouping, we can focus on the new plan we develop to help us get what we want. If we don't learn to regroup and refocus, we tend to feel like we are on a hamster wheel of treadmill of life, going nowhere fast.

2. **It's a way of getting on the right path.** Rejection can give you valuable feedback. Learning where you went wrong (if, in fact, you did; more on that shortly) gives you ways to improve in the future.

3. **Rejection builds resilience and perseverance.** Nelson Mandela once said, "Do not judge me by my success, judge me by how many times I fell down and got back up again." Success is not a straight line from here to there. It is a twisted path with its ups and downs. As we experience the setbacks, we need to use them as set-ups for the good that is to come our way. The setbacks and wrong turns create the resilience and perseverance needed to get to where we want to go.

4. **It's a reason to be proud of yourself.** If you are rejected, it means you are trying. For every person who is rejected, there are many more who didn't try to begin with—but you did.

5. **Occasional letdowns make success sweeter.** If all we ever experienced was success, we would begin to normalize it and grow comfortable with it. Maybe even expect it a little too much and think we are entitled to it. Letdowns, rejections, setbacks, mistakes, and failures are all meant to help

us appreciate real success when we experience it. That is why letdowns make success even sweeter.

Many studies have shown that successful people deal with rejection differently than others do. One such study conducted by Stanford University revealed that people who were able to handle rejection positively demonstrated higher levels of resilience and perseverance—traits that are essential for achieving long-term success.

Imagine being rejected by fourteen publishers. That was the reality for Stephen King and his first novel, *Carrie.* He went on to become one of the best-selling authors of all time. This is a prime example of turning rejection into fuel for success.

"He who fears he shall suffer, already suffers what he fears."
—Michel de Montaigne

In 2008, Brian Acton applied for jobs at Twitter and Facebook but was rejected by both. Instead of accepting defeat, he teamed up with his friend Jan Koum to develop a cross-platform messaging app called WhatsApp. In 2014, Facebook bought WhatsApp for $19 billion! Rejection ultimately led Acton to co-found one of the most successful tech start-ups in recent history.

Rejection often feels like the end of the world, but in reality, it's just the beginning of finding your true path.

Now let's talk about concrete steps you can take to turn your next *no* into an opportunity.

How to Bounce Back From Rejection

1. **Don't take it personally**. Understand that there are many possible reasons someone might say no. Rejection can be subjective; it's not always about you.

2. **Document what happened and learn from it.** Put yourself in the shoes of the person who rejected you, and think about whether there is something you could have done differently to get you closer to a yes. Then fix those things. It might mean changing your approach or acquiring new skills.

3. **Try again.** Sometimes, as I alluded to earlier, you didn't do anything wrong, and you simply need to try again when the timing is better.

4. **Keep emotions in check.** It's natural to feel disappointed, but don't let it cloud your judgment.

5. **Seek support.** Talk with a mentor, friend, or counselor who can provide perspective and encouragement.

6. **Stay focused on other opportunities.** Don't dwell too much on one rejection—keep exploring new avenues. The only sure way to avoid rejection is to quit trying, but the pain of regret often outweighs the pain of rejection.

> *"The righteous cry out, and the Lord hears them; he delivers them from all their troubles. The Lord is close to the brokenhearted and saves those who are crushed in spirit. The righteous person may have many troubles, but the Lord delivers him from them all; he protects all his bones, not one of them will be broken."*
> —Psalms 34:17–20 NIV

Rejections are inevitable. What matters is how you choose to respond to them. And remember, every successful person has faced their fair share of rejections. Walt Disney was fired from his first job at a newspaper because they thought he wasn't creative enough! And Colonel Sanders had his recipe rejected over a thousand times before someone finally said yes! Every *no* brings you closer to that eventual *yes*.

So next time you face a *no*, smile at it, learn from it, and move forward—because a *yes* might just be around the corner.

Reflection Questions

1. What stands out to you in this lesson on handling rejection?

2. Why is it important for you to better handle the rejections you face?

3. What will you do to handle rejections better as you move forward?

Conquer Self-Doubt

*"I have self-doubt. I have insecurity. I have fear of failure. I
have nights when I show up at the arena and I'm like, 'My
back hurts, my feet hurt, my knees hurt. I don't have it. I
just want to chill.' We all have self-doubt. You don't deny
it, but you also don't capitulate to it. You embrace it."*
—Kobe Bryant

Let's face it—we all experience doubts about our abilities
and worth from time to time. It is a common human phenomenon that can be as paralyzing as quicksand if not properly managed.

However, when embraced and channeled properly, this same
self-doubt can become a stepping stone towards success.

Self-doubt can be your worst enemy or best
friend, depending on how you handle it.

Overcoming self-doubt is much like navigating through a
dark tunnel with the hope of seeing light at its end. The darkness
represents your fears and insecurities, while the light symbol-
izes confidence, success, and fulfillment.

To navigate successfully through this tunnel of self-doubt, there are several steps you need to undertake.

How to Overcome Self-Doubt

1. **Stop making excuses.** Excuses are defensive shields protecting us from facing our inadequacies head-on. They also keep us from taking risks, learning, and making breakthroughs. To overcome self-doubt, you must discard excuses and confront your insecurities bravely.

2. **Be aware of your five people.** Jim Rohn once said, "You are the average of the five people you spend the most time with." Surround yourself with individuals who believe in you even when you doubt yourself. Their faith in your abilities will eventually rub off on you.

3. **Raise your self-awareness.** Being aware of your strengths and weaknesses is essential for personal growth and development. Knowing what areas need improvement helps reduce feelings of inadequacy and enhances your confidence in your capabilities.

4. **Be kind to yourself.** You are human, and it's okay to make mistakes. Rather than beat yourself up over failures, learn from them and move forward.

5. **Stop asking for validation.** Seeking others' approval for every decision fosters dependency and fuels self-doubt. Once you've done your research (which can include seeking advice from knowledgeable people), trust your judgment and make decisions independently.

6. **Don't put your plans on blast.** Talking about your plans to everyone under the sun can trick your brain into thinking you've already accomplished them, leading to a lack of motivation to follow through. Of course you may need to discuss ideas with mentors or knowledgeable people from whom you are seeking advice. But for the most part, keep your plans to yourself until you've achieved them.

7. **Trust your values.** When you let your values guide your actions, you feel more confident in your decision-making abilities and experience less self-doubt.

8. **"Start shipping."** According to Seth Godin, when you begin executing your ideas as opposed to overthinking or second-guessing them, you're "shipping." It means moving past the fear of failure or judgment that often accompanies self-doubt.

"Finally, be strong in the Lord and in his mighty power."
—Ephesians 6:10 NIV

Ephesians 6:10 inspires me because it is a reminder that we possess an inner strength capable of overcoming any obstacle—including self-doubt—if we tap into our faith and courage.

The journey might not be easy, but rest assured that once you emerge from the tunnel's end, the light will be worth every step taken in darkness.

Reflection Questions

1. What stands out to you in this lesson on overcoming self-doubt?

2. How has self-doubt held you back in the past?

3. What can you commit to in order to overcome your self-doubt?

Never Quit

"I shed a tear when I meet somebody who always quits. Reliable people are so rare in this world."
—Benson Bruno

"If you quit once, it becomes a habit. Never quit."
—Michael Jordan

"Most people who succeed in the face of seemingly impossible conditions are people who simply don't know how to quit."
—Robert Schuller

"Effort only fully releases its reward after a person refuses to quit."
—Napoleon Hill

The Benefits of Quitting

None!

Never quit—nothing good comes from quitting on your dreams.

Scientifically speaking, research has found that our brains are wired for survival, not success. This means when faced with adversity, our brain's default reaction is to retreat or quit.

However, there is immense power in persistence.

Imagine planting a seed, then impatiently digging it up every few minutes to see if it has grown. This constant disruption would prevent the seed from sprouting roots and eventually bearing fruit. Similarly, constantly quitting and restarting will only hinder your growth and success.

The benefits of quitting:

NONE!

Real growth is impossible if you are unwilling to persist. Imagine participating in a marathon with no prior training or experience. As the race begins, everyone else rushes past, leaving you behind. Exhausted and outpaced, you feel like giving up.

How do we keep going when everything seems stacked against us? Here are five actionable steps.

How to Resist the Urge to Quit

1. **Connect to your purpose.** Identify what truly motivates you—your "why"—and then align your actions towards achieving that purpose. When the going gets tough, your purpose will keep you going.

2. **Change your story.** See challenges not as barriers but as opportunities to grow. If you quit, you won't grow—so see if there is anything you can improve about your approach, and

keep going.

3. **Divide and conquer.** If a task seems so daunting that you want to quit, split it into achievable steps. The incremental successes will motivate you not to give up.

4. **Try cognitive restructuring activities such as positive affirmations and visualization.** When you want to quit, every tool you can bring to bear will help you feel more in control and less like giving up.

5. **Celebrate small successes.** It's important to acknowledge even the smallest of victories, as they fuel motivation and build momentum.

6. **Find support.** Ask a mentor for advice, or pair up with a friend who is going through a similar trial and be comrades-in-arms. If you find yourself succumbing to the temptation of quitting easily despite trying these strategies, it might be time for some professional help—a life coach or a therapist could provide valuable guidance.

> *"Let us not become weary in doing good, for at the proper time we will reap a harvest if we do not give up."*
> —Galatians 6:9 NIV

Pursue your dreams relentlessly. Remember that most successful people have faced times when they felt like giving up, but part of what set them apart was their unyielding spirit and refusal to quit. Nothing worthwhile comes easy, but with the help of the strategies listed above, you can do it. Keep pushing forward!

Reflection Questions

1. What stands out to you in this lesson on quitting?

2. What would it mean to you if you never quit on yourself and your goals again in your life?

3. What is one step you can take to ensure you will never quit on yourself?

LESSON 11

Be Consistent

*"Success isn't always about greatness. It's about consistency.
Consistent hard work leads to success. Greatness will come."*
—Dwayne Johnson

Initiating any new venture, be it a business, learning a new skill, or embarking on a health and fitness journey, is often fraught with excitement. However, after the initial thrill wears off and reality sets in, the real challenge begins.

That's where consistency plays its part.

In essence, consistency is all about repetition tempered with discipline—repeating beneficial actions regularly even when immediate results aren't visible.

Success in your endeavors isn't necessarily about having an extraordinary idea or talent. It's about being reliable and consistent. Aristotle once said, "We are what we repeatedly do. Excellence, then, is not an act but a habit." This simple yet profound statement underlines the essence of personal improvement—consistency in action and thought.

A person who practices playing piano every
day for fifteen minutes will eventually
outperform someone who spends hours at the
keyboard but does so only sporadically.

The Benefits of Being Consistent

1. **Consistency builds momentum.** Considerable force is needed to start any endeavor. However, just like pushing a car, once things get rolling, the effort required is less.

2. **It establishes credibility.** When you're consistent with what you do or say, people start trusting you more because they know what they can expect from you.

3. **It aids in mastering skills.** Consistent practice helps you get better at any skill due to muscle memory and the laying down of new neural pathways in the brain. Plus, the more often you practice a skill, the easier it is to measure your progress and the faster you can identify areas for improvement.

4. **It makes you more efficient.** Consistent efforts lead to habits, which make you more efficient over time.

Evidence of the effectiveness of consistency isn't hard to find. The average person trying to lose weight won't see noticeable changes after working out for just a week. But if they work out consistently for months, the results will be significant.

Consider famous authors like Stephen King or musicians like The Beatles. Their success didn't come overnight but was the result of years of consistent work and practice.

"Long-term consistency trumps short term intensity."
—Bruce Lee

When applied to our lives, consistency can lead to profound changes over time. A daily reading habit can turn into large knowledge over the years; regular savings can accumulate into wealth, and so on.

A study conducted at University College London found that it takes an average of sixty-six days for a new behavior to become automatic. That's about two months of consistently doing something before it becomes a habit!

Consistency is the key link between goals and accomplishment. It gets you from where you are to where you want to be.

Consistency isn't perfection. It's more about progress than getting everything right all the time. Nor is it about being rigid. Flexibility is crucial for adapting to unexpected circumstances while sticking to your end goal.

Consistency requires commitment to stay on course even when things get tough. It's easier when driven by purpose: Knowing why you're doing what you're doing makes staying consistent easier.

Now let's move on to actionable steps.

How to Be Consistent

1. **Start small.** Begin with manageable tasks or activities that don't overwhelm you, then work your way up over time.

2. **Set clear goals.** Know what you're working towards and break it down into smaller, achievable targets.

3. **Create a routine.** Incorporate the desired activity into your daily weekly routine. According to a study published in the *European Journal of Social Psychology*, people who performed an activity consistently in the same context (time and place) were more likely to form habits faster compared to those who varied their routine.

4. **Track your progress.** Keep a record of your actions to visualize your progress and stay motivated.

5. **Stay accountable.** Sharing your goals and your progress with a friend can motivate you to stay on track.

6. **Celebrate small wins.** Reward yourself for consistency to reinforce positive behavior.

> *"Therefore, my dear brothers and sisters, stand firm. Let nothing move you. Always give yourselves fully to the work of the Lord, because you know that your labor in the Lord is not in vain."*
> —1 Corinthians 15:58 NIV

Remember, success is not an overnight phenomenon—it's the sum total of consistent efforts over time. So start today, do something beneficial consistently, and watch as the magic unfolds in due course.

Reflection Questions

1. What stands out to you in this lesson on consistency?

2. What would you achieve if you were to become more consistent in all areas of your life?

3. What is one step you can take to become more consistent?

LESSON 12

Persevere

*"Perseverance is not a long race—it is many
short races one after another."*
—Walter Elliot

The path to success is often described as a marathon. I prefer to think of it as a series of sprints, each presenting its unique challenges and obstacles.

Either way, the path to success is long, and it requires perseverance, defined as tenacity or doggedness—the act of sticking with something even when the odds are stacked against you.

Nature provides marvelous examples of perseverance. Large species of bamboo may spend five or more years establishing their root systems, then sprout upward dramatically within six weeks. The nymphs of some periodic cicadas stay underground for seventeen years before emerging to develop into adults. Sometimes apparent inactivity or slow progress actually lays foundations for rapid growth later on.

In his book *21 Irrefutable Laws of Leadership*, John Maxwell talks about four combinations:

1. Right Action, Wrong Time

2. Wrong Action, Right Time

3. Wrong Action, Wrong Time

4. Right Action, Right Time

In other words, you can take the right action and still fail simply because the timing was wrong. This is why perseverance is so important.

> Perseverance doesn't mean blindly charging ahead, ignoring feedback, or refusing to adapt. Instead, it involves learning from your mistakes and failures, adjusting your strategies and methods accordingly, but never giving up on your ultimate goal.

Perseverance involves learning from your mistakes and failures, adjusting your strategies and methods accordingly, but never giving up on your ultimate goal.

How to Persevere

1. **Set clear goals**. We have mentioned setting goals several times already in this book. So it can't get lost on any of us how important it is to have goals that are clear, specific, measurable, attainable, relevant and timed. Goals give us hope for a better future. Hope helps us keep going and motivates us to persevere.

2. **Break goals down into manageable steps**. Once we have clear goals, we can create a plan for how we are going to achieve them. Within the plan will be the activities and steps we need to take. Recently, I bench-pressed 200 pounds for the first time in well over 25 years. Six months ago, I was

bench-pressing about 135 pounds. The steps I put in front of me were to increase my bench press weight every month by at least 10 pounds. So that would be my example of manageable steps because a 10-pound increase over some months is far more manageable than a 65-pound increase in 1 month.

3. **Celebrate small victories**. One of the biggest mistakes people make is not celebrating the small victories. Victories and celebrations make us feel good about ourselves and our accomplishments. Feeling good builds momentum. Be careful, though, that you don't celebrate for too long, as this may stop you from taking the actions required to continue to where you want to go and you will sabotage your own momentum. I like to match the celebration to the victories.

4. **Learn from setbacks**. Without learning from our setbacks, we are bound to make the same mistakes again. Continuing to make the same mistakes again will discourage us and cause us to want to quit. Quitting kills perseverance instantly.

5. **Get support from a friend or mentor**. An accountability partner is crucial in perseverance. Most of us don't want to disappoint the people we love, so having to check in with them or having them check in on us will keep us pushing forward.

6. **Employ strategies such as mindfulness and visualization to support your progress**. I believe strongly in visualizing our success before we achieve it. I once heard an interview with Bodie Miller, an American skier. After years of setbacks, mostly due to his own mistakes, he won an Olympic Gold Medal. Upon winning the gold medal, he immediately had a camera and microphone thrust into his face and the reporter asked, "What does it feel like to have finally won this elusive gold medal?" The first words out of his mouth were, "Exactly

as I had envisioned it...!" He believed strongly in visualization, and so do I. I regularly visualize success in my life activities. When I do, and can see success as mine, it gives me the courage to try anything. I want to encourage you to do the same.

Remember: Every step forward, no matter how small, brings us closer to our destination. Therefore:

> *"Let perseverance finish its work so that you may*
> *be mature and complete, not lacking anything."*
> *—James 1:4 NIV*

Reflection Questions

1. What stands out to you in this lesson on perseverance?

2. Why would it be important to you to become better at perseverance?

3. What is one step you can take to grow in your perseverance?

Conclusion

Thank you for taking the time to read through all 12 lessons. This book is really a little guide that can result in big successes as you practice the lessons.

As I said at the beginning of the book, it's not about knowing these lessons but about implementing each of them in your daily activities.

The four characteristics that have helped me the most to live out these lessons are commitment, discipline, consistency, and courage.

Commitment to begin and stick with my success image and success drivers even when things aren't going my way.

Discipline to live out the lessons. It helps when my purpose and passion are aligned with the activities I am doing to be disciplined.

Consistency to show up every day regardless of how I feel or what hardships are present in my life.

Courage to take another step or try again at something I have failed at.

It would bring me great joy to hear that, in some small or big way, this book helps you to live the life of your dreams.

Resources

have assembled some of my best resources, books, & podcasts to help you on your journey. The extent or level of resources you will want or need depends on your goals and dreams and the amount of help you need.

www.Project1202.com

- Over 200 Growth Lessons
- DISC Behavioral Style Assessment
- Coaching
- Digital Products
- Speaking
- Training

Recommended Reading List

- The 15 Invaluable Laws of Growth by John C. Maxwell
- The 21 Laws of Leadership by John C. Maxwell
- Develop the Leader Within You 2.0 by John C. Maxwell
- High Performance Habits by Brendon Burchard

- <u>The Chase–Success, Motivation, and the Scriptures</u> by William H. Cook

- <u>The 4:8 Principle</u> by Tommy Newberry

About the Author

Rich Lohman is a celebrated author in the Leadership and Personal Development niche, renowned for his profound insights and practical approach to success. His book, *The Little Guide to BIG Success: 12 Straightforward Lessons to Succeed at Anything!* is a testament to his dedication to helping others achieve their potential.

Rich's writing is characterized by his ability to distill complex concepts into easily digestible content. He believes that success isn't an overnight phenomenon but a result of consistent effort, resilience, and an unwavering commitment to personal growth.

His work embodies this belief, providing readers with a roadmap for success that is both realistic and inspiring.

His passion for leadership and personal development shines through in every page of his book. Rich has spent countless hours researching the intricacies of effective leadership and the nuances of personal growth.

His commitment to understanding these subjects deeply informs his writing, making it rich with knowledge and practical advice.

In *The Little Guide to BIG Success: 12 Straightforward Lessons to Succeed at Anything!*, Rich shares invaluable insights into the journey towards success. He emphasizes that success is not about quick fixes or shortcuts but about showing up every day, working hard, embracing failure as an opportunity for growth, facing challenges head-on, and never giving up.

Rich's vision extends beyond just sharing knowledge—he aims to empower his readers with tools they can use in their journey towards becoming highly successful people. He encourages them to embrace their unique paths and cultivate resilience in the face of adversity.